AFTERNOONS WITH MY NONNI

BY AMANDA DI PANCRAZIO
ILLUSTRATED BY MARIIA STEPANOVA

FOR NONNA ANNA & NONNO VIRGINIO -
MISSING AFTERNOONS, MORNINGS,
AND NIGHTS WITH YOU.

Once a week, we visit Nonna and Nonno. They're my grandparents!

"Buongiorno, Nonna! Come stai?
Hi Grandma! How are you?"

"Ciao, amore! Hi, my love! Nonno and I are just finishing up a game of cards."

"What game are you playing?"

"Scopa. It's a game that you play with Italian playing cards. Whoever has the most points when there are no more cards wins. SCOPA! I win. Let's go to the park!"

"How do you play bocce?"

"It's like a game of darts, but with balls. You start by throwing the small ball, and then take turns tossing the bigger balls as close to it as possible."

"I'm preparing ravioli with ricotta - a type of cheese - and polpette, which are meatballs.

First you drop spoonfuls of ricotta on a sheet of dough, and cover that with another sheet of dough.

Finally, you press and cut around each ball of ricotta to make your ravioli. And then you cook them!"

"What are those?"

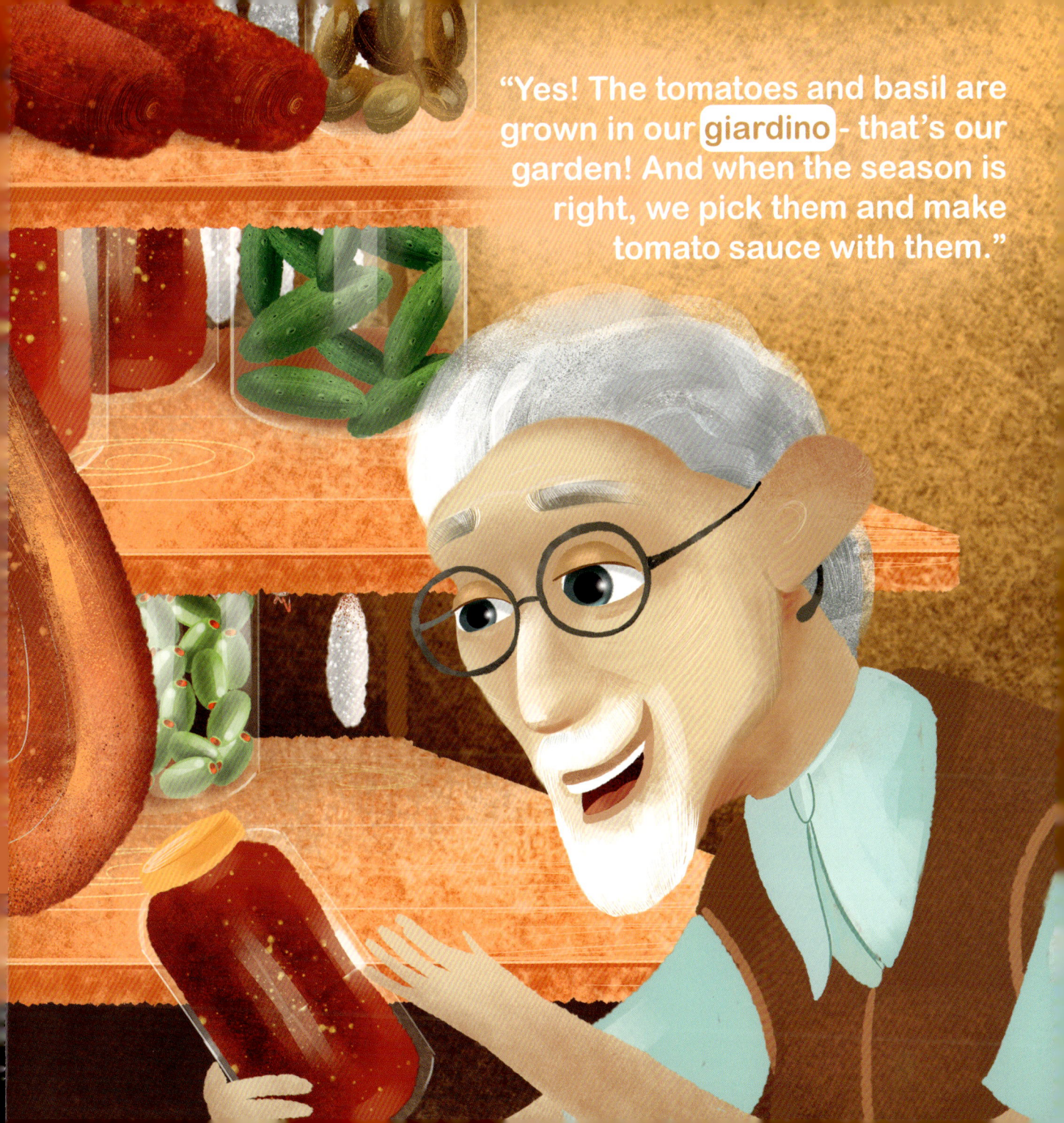